Young Musician

Playing the

Trumpet
and
Brass

Paul Archibald

Franklin Watts
London • Sydney

INTRODUCTION

Welcome to the exciting world of the trumpet! As you will discover when you start playing, the trumpet has a unique sound, brilliant and beautiful. It can play very high and very low notes. These things take many hours of practice to master, but when you have worked through this book you will have a solid foundation on which to build.

The trumpet is a member of the brass family, like the trombone, tuba and French horn. It is basically a length of hollow metal tube, opening out into a bell at one end, and with a mouthpiece at the other. When air passes through the tube it vibrates and sound is produced.

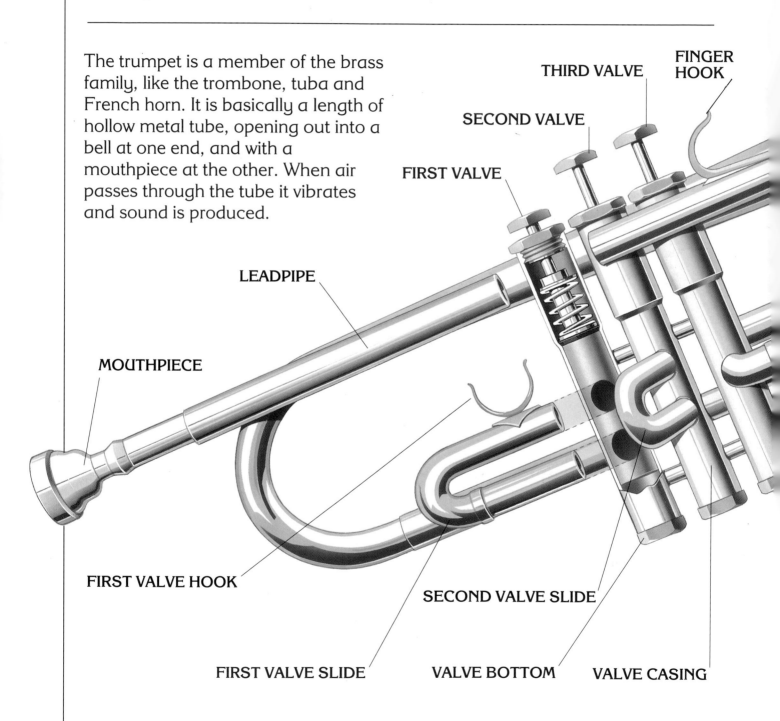

THIRD VALVE

FINGER HOOK

SECOND VALVE

FIRST VALVE

LEADPIPE

MOUTHPIECE

FIRST VALVE HOOK

FIRST VALVE SLIDE

SECOND VALVE SLIDE

VALVE BOTTOM

VALVE CASING

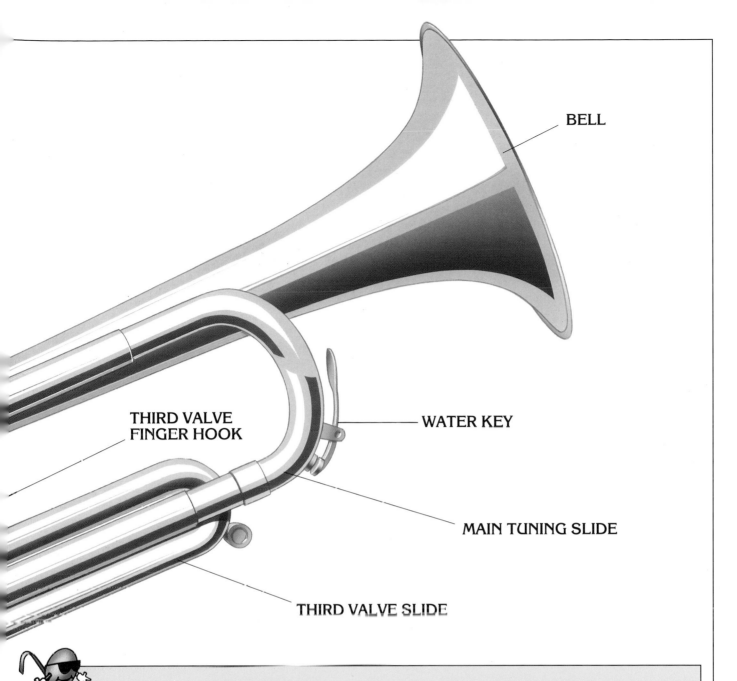

BELL

THIRD VALVE
FINGER HOOK

WATER KEY

MAIN TUNING SLIDE

THIRD VALVE SLIDE

THE VALVE – HOW IT WORKS

Air directed into the mouthpiece of the trumpet passes down the length of the instrument to emerge at the bell, as shown below. The valve, shown on the right, is a device that allows air to pass along a further length of tubing called a valve slide. For instance, when the third valve is pressed down, the holes in the valve allow air to pass through the third valve slide, as shown above. This lowers the pitch of the instrument, since the longer the tube through which the air passes, the lower the note. As you can see in the main illustration above, the three valve slides are of different lengths: short, medium and long. This allows the pitch of the instrument to be lowered gradually.

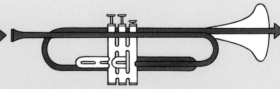

GETTING STARTED

Your trumpet should come supplied with a separate mouthpiece. It should be enclosed in a sturdy case, as it is very easy to damage metal instruments. A mute will affect the sound produced by your trumpet.

HOLDING THE TRUMPET – THE LEFT HAND

The trumpet should be held with your left hand around the valve casing. Your left thumb should be placed on the first valve casing, with your fourth finger through the finger hook (if there is one). The weight of the instrument should be on your forefinger, under the bell.

THE RIGHT HAND

Put the little finger of your right hand in the finger hook, as shown in the photograph below. Place the middle three fingers on the valves and place your thumb on the valve casing. Your right hand should not carry the weight of the instrument, and should remain as relaxed as possible.

STANDING POSITION

Make sure both feet are flat on the floor and a few inches apart. Keep your whole body, including your head, as straight as possible. Think of the trumpet's leadpipe as an extension of your nose and try to keep the bell up!

SITTING POSITION

Find a chair that allows you to put both feet on the floor. Sit in the middle of the chair, with your body as straight as possible. Try not to slouch against the back of the chair. Keep as relaxed as you can, and try to prevent the bell from drooping!

TIP:
If you find the trumpet heavy and your shoulders start to ache – put the instrument down, and lift your shoulders up and down as fast as possible. They will feel a lot better afterwards.

CARING FOR YOUR TRUMPET

Taking good care of your trumpet is important. When you finish playing, remove the mouthpiece, and put the instrument back in the case. Oil the valves every few days with trumpet valve oil. Make sure that all the slides can move. Apply trumpet slide grease or cream if necessary. At least every two weeks, rinse the instrument out with washing up liquid and hot water. If you take the valves off, lay them out in order, so they don't get mixed up. Dry the instrument with a soft cloth.

EMBOUCHURE

The shape that you make with your lips when playing the trumpet is called an embouchure (pronounced om-boo-sure). It is the basis of all your playing, so it is important to get it right from the beginning. With your lips in the correct position, you will produce sound through the trumpet, not by blowing, but by "buzzing".

THE "BUZZ"

If you take two blades of grass, place them alongside your two thumbs and blow between them, you should be able to make a loud squeaking sound. This happens because the two blades of grass are vibrating together very quickly. When playing the trumpet the principle is similar, but we don't use grass – we use our lips!

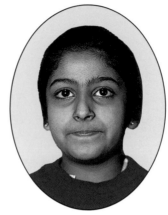

Look at the photograph, make the same shape with your lips, and try to produce a buzzing sound, like a wasp. It might take a little while to get the hang of it, but keep trying. Push the corners of your mouth down as shown here.

When you are confident with buzzing, place the mouthpiece on your lips as shown below. Place it in the middle of your mouth, with half on your upper lip and half on your lower lip. As you put the mouthpiece to your lips don't change from the "buzz" position.

Don't put the mouthpiece towards either side of your mouth, as shown below, only in the middle. Don't put the mouthpiece too low on your top lip – make sure you have half the mouthpiece on top, half on the bottom. Never blow your cheeks out!

FIRST NOTES

At last we are ready to go! Place the mouthpiece back on the trumpet. Start "buzzing", then place the mouthpiece in the centre of your embouchure and your first note should be heard. It will probably be middle C. Don't worry if it doesn't work straight away, you will soon get used to the feel of your lips vibrating.

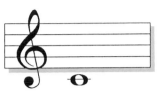

Middle C is called an open note because none of the valves are pressed down. In music it looks like this.

Press the first and third valves and buzz for the note D. D is above C and appears in the space above it.

Press the first and second valves to sound the note E. It sounds above D and appears on the line above it.

Trumpets and horns date back to before Roman times. They were used by soldiers in battle, for ceremonies and for hunting. Early "natural" trumpets had no valves (right), and could only play a limited range of notes. Bach and Handel wrote very high music for the natural trumpet.

EARLY NATURAL TRUMPETS

READING MUSIC

Written music can look complicated, but it's really quite easy. Notes are represented by black and white dots arranged on five lines called a stave. The stave is divided into units of time called "bars", and the treble clef at the start indicates the pitch of the stave. The position of the notes on the stave tells us how high or low they are.

WRITTEN MUSIC

Musical notes are named after the letters of the alphabet, from A to G. After G the letters begin again. Reading from the bottom upwards, the names of the notes on the lines in the treble clef are E G B D F (try remembering – Every Good Boy Deserves Favours). The notes on the spaces between the lines of the treble clef spell F A C E. The treble clef is the curly symbol which appears at the start of the music.

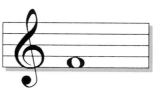

Here are two new notes to learn. The note F sounds above E. Buzz and press down the first valve.

G is an open note like C, with no valves down. G is higher than C – make sure you can hear the difference.

Now try all five notes:

Once you feel confident playing five notes, try the next exercise, which adds on three more notes – A, B and high C. The new fingerings appear beneath the notes. This is called a scale. It consists of seven notes followed by the original note one octave (or eight notes) higher. Play up the scale and then try coming down. Then try it from memory .

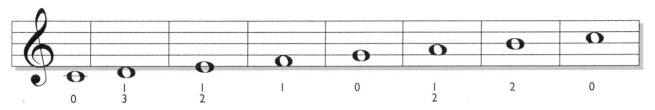

Don't worry if you find it difficult to play all the notes. Just play the ones you find easy – the rest will come, the more familiar you are with the instrument. If you can play all the notes, try the exercise below. Can you name all the notes that appear in this piece?

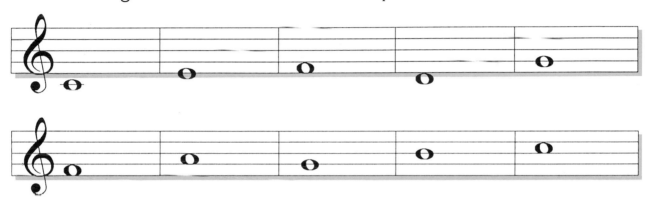

JOSEPH HAYDN

Joseph Haydn was born in 1732, in Austria. His talent for music was soon obvious, and he was admitted as a boy chorister at St Stephen's Cathedral in Vienna. In 1761, he was employed by a wealthy nobleman, Prince Esterházy, near Vienna. This post allowed him to compose many symphonies, string quartets and instrumental concertos. A concerto is a piece for a solo instrument accompanied by the orchestra. Haydn's last concerto was written in 1796 for the trumpet. It is the finest work ever written for the instrument.

ADDING THE BEAT

If you listen to your watch or clock, you will notice that it has a very regular "tick" or beat. The same applies to most of the music we play, but although the beat remains the same, the rhythm or pattern of notes constantly changes.

LONG AND SHORT NOTES

Longer and shorter notes are represented by different symbols in written music. The longest note shown here is the whole-note, or semibreve, and the shortest is the eighth-note, or quaver. In terms of time, each of the notes shown here is worth two of the ones directly below it. Try counting or clapping each line: count four for a semibreve and two

One whole-note (semibreve) =

Two half-notes (minims) =

Four quarter-notes (crotchets) =

Eight eighth-notes (quavers)

for a minim. The exercises below use the notes you have learnt, with some of the new rhythms or note lengths. Count or clap them through before trying them on your trumpet.

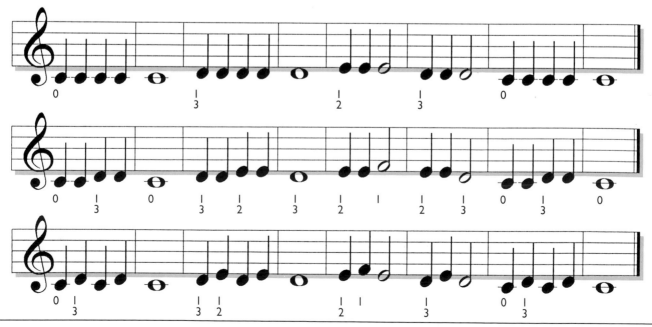

RESTS

As you have probably discovered, all this playing is quite exhausting! However, help is at hand, as music often has silences, called rests, built in. Different rest symbols correspond to all the note values you have met, as shown on the right. Rests can be very useful when we have to breathe. Try the exercises below, that include some of these new symbols.

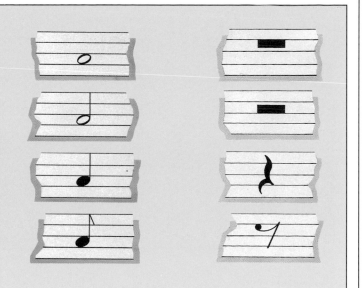

CLASSICAL TRUMPET

The trumpet as we know it today started to take shape with the invention of the valve in the early part of the 19th century. This meant that the trumpet could play more notes, and not be restricted to just a few. Composers such as Berlioz, Wagner, Ravel and Mahler began to write more complicated music for the instrument. As the music developed, so the trumpet family grew, and instruments of different lengths, sizes and even different numbers of valves were invented.

TONGUING

The tongue plays a very important rôle in trumpet-playing. Not only does it provide the start of each note for us, but it also regulates the pitch of the note. It decides whether the note will be high or low. When playing the trumpet, your tongue moves up inside your mouth naturally as you sound higher notes.

NOTE PRODUCTION

The two most common ways to produce a note are: positioning the tip of the tongue behind the upper teeth to say "ta", shown right, or putting the tip of the tongue behind the bottom teeth and using the middle of the tongue to say "da". Move the tongue quickly to give a clear, crisp "attack".

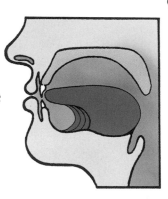

PITCH AND TONGUING

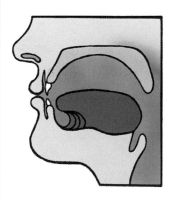

The position of your tongue affects the pitch of the note. When you say "Ah" loudly your tongue will be positioned low in your mouth (left). This is where your tongue will be when playing middle C. If you say "Eee" loudly, your tongue moves higher in your mouth (right). This is its position for high C.

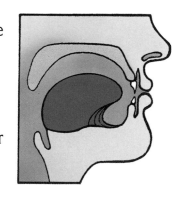

TIME SIGNATURES

At the beginning of each piece of music you will see two numbers, one on top of the other. This is called a time signature: the top number tells you how many beats there are in each bar.

The bottom number tells you how long each beat is. Three of the most common time signatures appear above. 2/4 time has two quarter-notes (crotchets) to a bar, or the equivalent in

notes of other time values. 3/4 time, with three quarter-notes, is used in waltzes and other music. 4/4 time, with four quarter-notes to a bar, is also known as common time.

RHYTHM PRACTICE

These exercises use different time signatures. As you play them, imagine the ticking of your watch, and try and play the correct note lengths. You can try clapping the rhythm before you play!

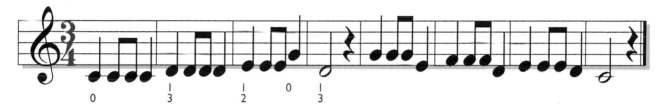

TONGUE-TWISTERS

Notes played in rapid succession can be very exciting. Rapid notes can be achieved either by double-tonguing, or by triple-tonguing. If you say the word "taka" quickly several times, you will produce a series of very fast sounds or notes. This is double-tonguing. If you say the word "tataka" quickly several times you get the same effect, but in groups of three. This is triple-tonguing. Trumpeter Wynton Marsalis (left) uses both methods of tonguing.

BREATHING

One of the most important things in trumpet playing is breathing. This may sound strange, because we are breathing all the time. But just as an engine provides power to a motor-car, so your breath supply provides the power for your trumpet playing.

Hold your hand in front of your mouth and cough. You will notice that the air is pushed out quickly. Put your other hand on your stomach. Your stomach will feel as though it is being pushed upwards. Now imagine blowing out all the candles on a birthday cake. Take a deep breath and push the air out as fast as you can. Make sure you can feel the "upward"

movement in your stomach. Practise this until you become used to the amount of air you are breathing in and pushing out. Try blowing up a balloon as extra practice! Now position yourself where you can see a clock. Play the notes below, holding each one for as long as possible. Take a deep breath and try to keep the sound steady. Can the sound you are making be improved?

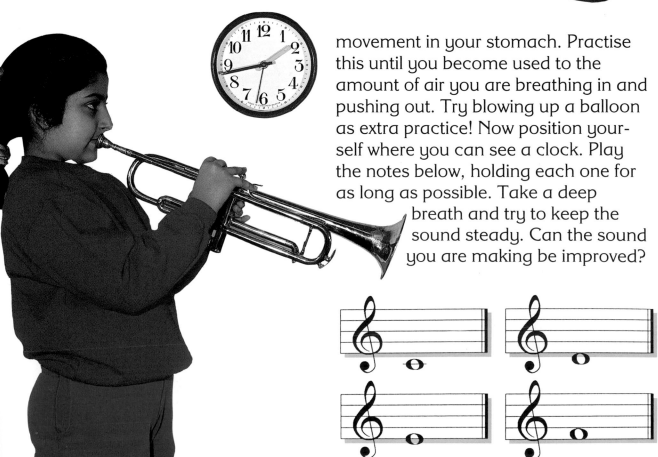

BAD HABITS

As you become more familiar with your trumpet, it is important to avoid bad habits. Always stand or sit correctly, keeping your shoulders and back straight (see page 7). Hold the trumpet correctly (page 6). Use only the tips of your right hand fingers to press the valves down. Make sure you are forming your embouchure in the centre of your mouth (page 8). Always start notes clearly and crisply (page 14).

PLAYING IN PUBLIC

When you eventually give your first performance, remember to take deep breaths, even before you play. Concentrate on the music, and don't upset yourself if you make a mistake – you are only human!

THOMAS HARPER (FATHER AND SON)

The two leading players of the natural trumpet in Britain during the 19th century were the two Thomas Harpers. Thomas Harper (senior) was in constant demand as a performer from about 1806, and played at all the principal concerts and festivals in London. Thomas Harper (junior), right, succeeded his father and became a big celebrity too. Both musicians played a version of the natural trumpet called a "slide" trumpet.

SHARPS AND FLATS

The eight notes in the scale on page 11 are natural notes, the white keys on a piano. That scale is C major, because it starts on C. Scales which begin on other notes use sharps and flats, the black keys on the piano.

The sign for a sharp is shown on the left. A sharp raises the pitch of a note by half a tone. A flat sign is shown below left. It lowers the pitch of a note by half a tone. Sometimes sharps or flats appear in the "key signature" near the treble clef. They tell us the scale or key that the music is based on.

If no sharp or flat appears in the key signature, the key is C major. In the second line below, the key is G major, with F# in the key signature.

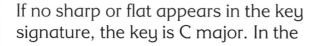

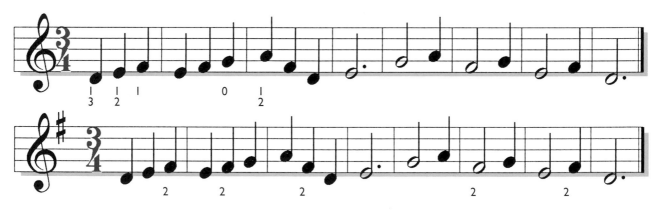

For every major key there is also a minor one. The first exercise below is in F major; the second is in D minor. Both have B♭ in the key signature.

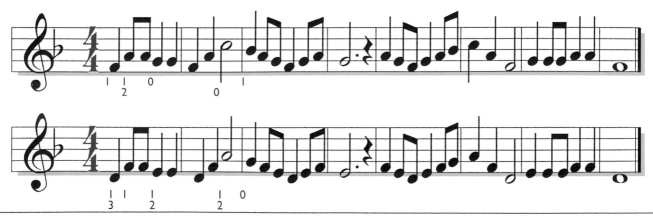

KEY SIGNATURES

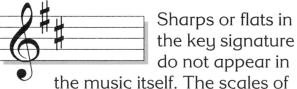

Sharps or flats in the key signature do not appear in the music itself. The scales of D major and B minor have $F^\#$ and $C^\#$ in the key signature.

The scales of B^b major and G minor both have B^b and E^b in their key signature. Remember to play these notes flat in the music itself.

Practise the exercises below, looking out for the key-signature. See if you can tell if they are written in a major or a minor key.

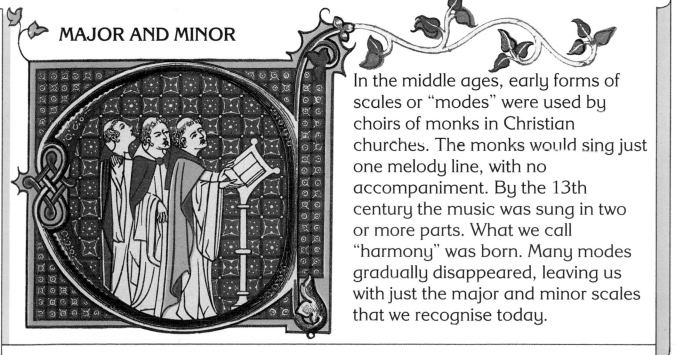

MAJOR AND MINOR

In the middle ages, early forms of scales or "modes" were used by choirs of monks in Christian churches. The monks would sing just one melody line, with no accompaniment. By the 13th century the music was sung in two or more parts. What we call "harmony" was born. Many modes gradually disappeared, leaving us with just the major and minor scales that we recognise today.

FINGER TECHNIQUE

Although there are only three valves on the trumpet, there are many different valve combinations. Some are very easy to play. Others are a little more difficult, and take longer to get used to. Move your fingers quickly and smoothly to a new valve combination, and make sure you don't sound a note whilst the valve is still half way down!

HAND MUSCLES

Hold your trumpet in your right hand as shown in the illustration below, and play the first and second valves alternately. You will find this change of fingering quite easy. If you try changing between the second and third valves you will find it much more difficult. This is because your third finger is rarely used on its own, and is much weaker than the others. The exercise below will help you to practise these difficult changes of fingering. Note that the music is in 3/4 time, with three quarter-notes in a bar. The two sharps in the key signature indicate the key of D major or B minor. Play the music and see if you can tell which key it is.

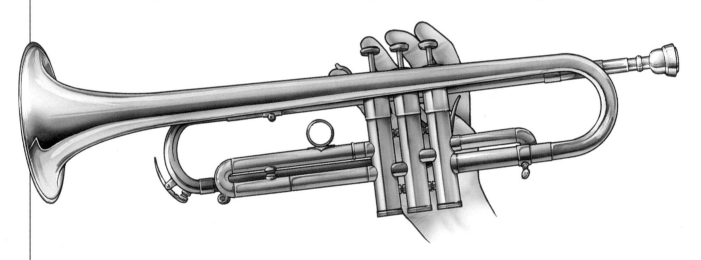

DOS AND DON'TS

Keep your right hand as relaxed as possible. Use the tips of the fingers to press down the valves. Never use the area underneath your knuckles. Always press the valve down quickly and smoothly. Press down combinations of valves together. Make sure the valves are down before you sound the note.

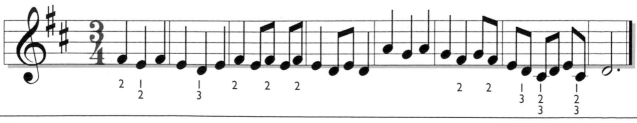

FIRST AND THIRD SLIDE

Some trumpets have move-able slides on their first and third valves. This is because some of the notes we play may be out of tune. By using these two slides it is possible to alter the tuning of the instrument when playing with these valves.

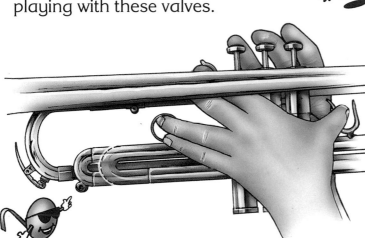

The illustration on the right shows the first valve slide, operated with your left thumb. The illustration on the left shows the third valve slide, operated with the left hand fourth finger. Play the exercises here without using the slides. Then play them again with both slides pulled out slightly – can you hear the difference?

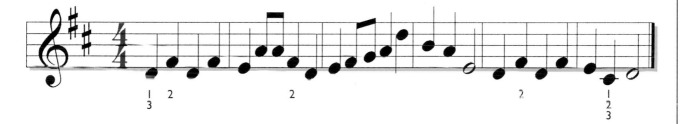

THE JAZZ TRUMPET

Since the beginning of this century, the trumpet has played a leading rôle in the development of jazz. Great jazz performers include Bix Biederbecke, a cornetist who made his impact in the 1920s. Dizzy Gillespie, right, helped develop the style of jazz in the 1940s called "Bepop". In the 1950s, trumpeter Miles Davis developed a more calm or "cool" approach to jazz, influencing another great jazz trumpeter, Chet Baker.

PRACTICE ROUTINE

Regular practice of the trumpet is important. You don't have to spend many hours practising – it is more useful to spend a short time every day. Because trumpeters use a very sensitive part of the body, the mouth, it is important to "warm up" properly.

REGULAR PRACTICE

Your daily practice routine should consist of a "warm-up", some scales, music set by your teacher, and any music that you really enjoy playing. Long notes are a good way of warming up, and improving your sound and stamina. Take a deep breath and see if you can hold a note for 16 seconds. If you find this is easy try 20, 30 or even 40 seconds!

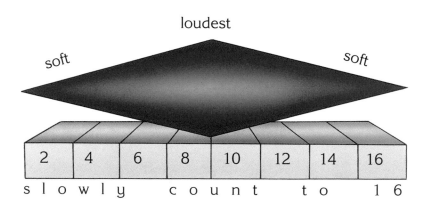

loudest

soft   soft

| 2 | 4 | 6 | 8 | 10 | 12 | 14 | 16 |

s l o w l y   c o u n t   t o   1 6

Your long notes should be shaped as shown here, starting quietly, getting louder, and then becoming quieter again. The exercise below also gets louder and softer, as shown by the symbols like hair pins.

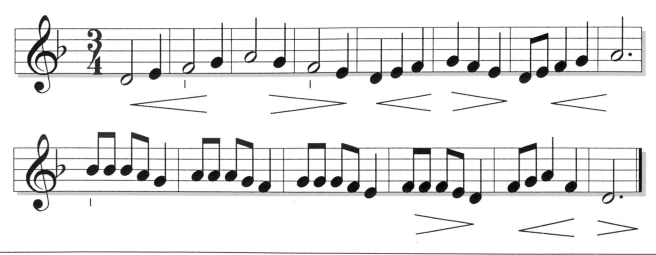

PLAYING A MELODY

The more you practise, the longer you will be able to play without becoming tired. As you improve, try to play melodies or pieces that are longer in length. Try the example below, in 3/4 time.

BRAHMS' LULLABY

HOW A TRUMPET IS MADE

Traditionally, all trumpets were hand-made by craftsmen, who shaped the trumpet bell by hand, beating it out on a steel form called a mandrel. The valves had to be cut to the correct length, then threaded, with the holes cut very carefully. The lengths of tubing to connect the bell and valves together were bent by heating the metal and hammering it into the correct shape. Today, these processes are usually done mechanically, but there are some craftsmen, like Martin Lechner, right, who still use traditional methods.

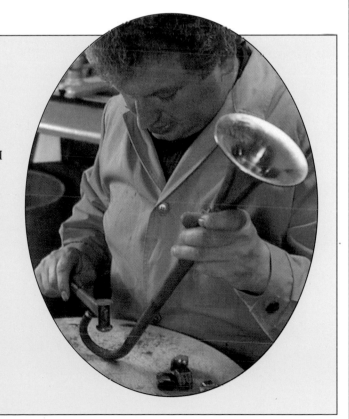

PLAYING TOGETHER

So far, all the music you have played has been for one trumpet. The real fun, however, starts when we play with others. A piece of music for two players is called a duet. If you have a friend who is also learning the trumpet (or a cornet, or even a clarinet) try the following exercise. Make sure that the two parts are equal in sound.

PLAYING A DUET

When playing a duet, you have to listen to your own sound, and also to the sound your partner is making.

Make sure that you play notes together and that you are "in tune" with each other.

Place the music stand between the two players.

Count yourselves in. Try to start and finish at the same time.

CANON

Four or more musicians playing together are an "ensemble". The exercise below, a canon, can be played by up to six people. The players join in the music one by one, each person beginning the piece two bars after the person before. The large C indicates common (4/4) time.

MUTES

A mute is a device which is placed in or over the trumpet bell to quieten, and to alter the sound. Three of the most common mutes are the "straight" mute, the "cup" mute, and the "harmon" or "wow-wow" mute. The "plunger" mute and "bucket" mute are sometimes used in jazz music to give a distinctive sound.

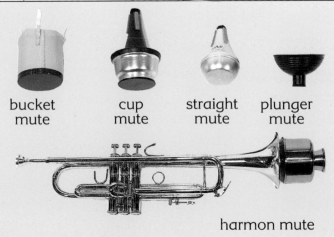

bucket mute

cup mute

straight mute

plunger mute

harmon mute

THE WORLD OF THE TRUMPET

The trumpet is a versatile instrument, used in many different kinds of music. It is heard in jazz, which was born at the start of the 20th century in New Orleans. It is also found in dance and military bands, and provides one of the most distinctive voices in the orchestra. Its relative, the cornet, is central to the brass band sound.

JAZZ BAND

French, Spanish, English, Italian, German and Slav influences all merged in early jazz. In a jazz band the cornet or trumpet, clarinet and trombone may all provide the melody, and are accompanied by other stringed or brass instruments.

BIG BANDS

An important development of the "swing" era of the 1930s was the big band. It consisted of large sections of trumpets, trombones and saxophones, with piano and drums adding to the melody and rhythm. It was through the big band that jazz became more popular.

THE ORCHESTRA

The brass section of the orchestra includes between two and five trumpets. It depends how many the composer wanted to perform the music. In the 18th century Mozart and Haydn wrote for only two trumpets. In the 19th and 20th centuries Mahler and Stravinsky wrote for five or even six trumpets.

FANFARE TRUMPETS

Fanfare trumpets are used to great effect at ceremonial occasions. Their bright and exciting sound is due to their elongated shape. The flag or emblem that is attached to the bell is for visual effect only, and makes no difference to the sound produced.

MILITARY BANDS

The brass section of a military band includes trumpets, cornets, French horns, euphoniums, trombones and tubas. The band will also contain a woodwind section, which includes oboes, flutes, clarinets, bassoons and saxophones.

THE CORNET AND THE BRASS BAND

The cornet developed as a result of the invention of the valve, and became a favourite with performers. It has a prominent rôle in the brass band. Brass bands were first formed during the 19th century in England, as a pastime for coal miners. The brass band consists of about 25 musicians, playing cornets, flugel horns, tenor horns, euphoniums and basses.

TRUMPET AND BRASS

Your trumpet is a member of a large family of trumpets, all named after the notes they correspond to on the piano. Your instrument is probably a B^b trumpet; there is also a C trumpet, a D trumpet and so on. The higher the trumpet, the shorter the instrument will be.

Try the following test with a piano. Play the first open note of the scale on page 11, your middle C, on your trumpet. Now play a B^b on the piano, or ask someone to play it for you. The notes should sound the same on both instruments. Your C equals the piano's B^b, so your trumpet is called a B^b trumpet. An E^b trumpet playing the same open note would sound the same as E^b on a piano.

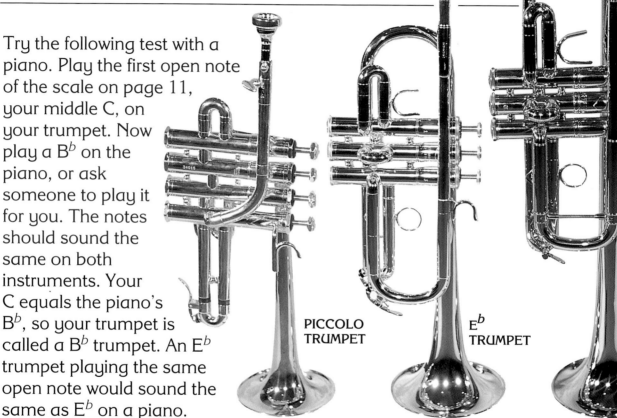

PICCOLO TRUMPET

E^b **TRUMPET**

C **TRUMPE**

ROTARY VALVE TRUMPET

The trumpets that are mostly used in Britain and the United States are known as piston trumpets. This name refers to the type of valve that is used in the instrument to produce a wider range of notes. In countries such as Germany and Austria, rotary valve trumpets are played instead. Rotary valves look similar to the valves used on French horns. Although they look very different from piston trumpets, rotary valve trumpets are played in exactly the same way.

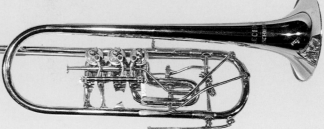

BRASS FAMILY

The **euphonium** (right) has a warm, deep, lyrical sound. The **trombone** (below) is the only modern brass instrument which uses a slide to produce a full range of notes.

The **sousaphone** was invented by John Philip Sousa for marching bands. The **tuba** (below) is another large member of the brass family. It was invented 150 years ago, for Russian military bands.

The **French horn** is a descendant of a hunting horn. It would measure five metres long if stretched out. The musician places one hand in the bell to improve the sound.

The **tenor horn** is used mainly in the brass band, where its warm, soft sound adds colour. You can expect to see three or four tenor horns in most brass bands.

LOUIS ARMSTRONG

Louis Armstrong was one of the strongest influences in the history of jazz. He learned to play whilst at reform school (he had been arrested for firing blanks from a pistol in the street). He was soon in demand as a cornetist, and eventually formed his own bands. His influence on many musicians is widely acknowledged.

COMPOSERS AND PERFORMERS

The natural trumpet has existed for many centuries. But it was not until the 17th century that composers started writing for it as a lyrical instrument. Over the last three centuries the repertoire of music for the instrument has become larger. Following the invention of the valve, music written for the trumpet has become much more varied.

JS Bach

Giuseppe Torelli (1658-1709) was one of the first to develop this style of composition. He wrote concertos, sinfonias and sonatas for the trumpet.

Antonio Vivaldi (1676-1741) wrote 400 concertos for various instruments. The important one for trumpeters is his

Richard Wagner

concerto for two trumpets which is now established as one of the major works in the instrument's repertoire.

Whilst these two composers were writing in Italy,

Georg Philipp Telemann (1681-1767) was composing in Germany. Amongst his compositions he included various concertos and suites for the trumpet.

The two composers who perfected the art of high trumpet writing were **Johann Sebastian Bach** (1685-1750) and **Georg Frideric Handel** (1685-1759). They often included two or three trumpets in their cantatas, oratorios, operas and other orchestral works, and these still represent some of the finest writing for

Gustav Mahler

Bix Biederbecke

the instrument to this day.

Towards the end of the 18th and beginning of the 19th century, manufacturers experimented with valves and with different types of trumpet. As a result, two magnificent concertos were written for the "keyed trumpet". One was by **Joseph Haydn** (1732-1809) and the other by **Johann Nepomuk Hummel** (1778-1837).

In the 19th century, composers such as **Hector Berlioz** (1803-69) **Richard Wagner**

Prior to the invention of the valve in the 19th century, composers were limited in their choice of notes for trumpet music, particularly when the instrument was played in the low register. It was noticed, however, that if the trumpet was played in its higher register, more notes could be played.

Composers of the baroque period (17th-early 18th century) exploited this to great effect, and the sound of the high trumpet is an important feature in this period of music.

Chet Baker

(1813-83) **Gustav Mahler** (1860-1911) and **Maurice Ravel** (1875-1937) all wrote wonderful music for the trumpet.

By the beginning of the 20th century, the valved trumpet was firmly established with composers and performers alike. Composers such as **Bohuslav Martinu** (1890-1959), **Jacques Ibert** (1890-1962) and **Paul Hindemith** (1895-1963) wrote music for trumpet and piano. Contemporary composers such as **Harrison Birtwistle** (born 1934) and **Peter Maxwell-Davies** have also written concertos for the instrument with orchestral accompaniment.

PERFORMERS

Over the past 300 years there have been many great *virtuoso* performers of the instrument. The 18th century included performers such as **Johann Ernst Altenburg**, who was also a composer, and **Anton Weidinger**, a Viennese trumpeter who gave some of the first performances of Haydn's trumpet concerto.

In England, during the 19th century, **Thomas Harper**, father and son, were the two most famous players, particularly of the English slide-trumpet. In France, **Jean-Baptiste Arban** and in America, **Herbert Clarke** gained reputations as great performers. Outstanding players of this century include **Bix Biederbecke**, **Maurice Andre**,

Hugh Masekela

Adolph Herseth, **Hakan Hardenberger**, **Miles Davis** and **John Faddis**. Jazz trumpeters include **Louis Armstrong**, **Chet Baker** and more recently **Hugh Masekela**.

GLOSSARY

Clef indicates the pitch of notes in written music.

Embouchure shaping the lips to the mouthpiece of a wind instrument.

Flat lowers a note by half a tone.

Harmonics or harmonic series a series of notes that can be played using the same valve or valves, or as open notes, without using any valves at all.

Key indicates the major or minor scale in which music is written.

Mute a device which quietens and alters the sound of an instrument.

Natural note that is not sharpened or flattened.

Octave an interval of eight natural notes. Two notes an octave apart have the same letter name.

Piston valve a device which allows the air column inside a trumpet to pass straight through the valve, but which when pressed down diverts the air along a length of tubing called a valve slide.

Pitch the highness or lowness of a note.

Rest a silent beat.

Rotary valve a device which allows the air column to pass straight through the valve, but is also able to divert the air by 45 degrees when rotated in its casing.

Scale the fixed pattern of notes on which most music is based.

Sharp raises a note by half a tone.

Stave the five horizontal lines on which musical notes are written.

INDEX

Photocredits

Abbreviations: l-left, r-right, b-bottom, t-top, c-centre, m-middle, ba-background
Front cover bm, 6 all, 7 all, 8 all, 9t, 10, 16 both, 17t, 18, 22, 24, 25 both, 27bl, 28 both, 29t, — Roger Vlitos. Front cover ba — Digital Stock. 9b, 19 — Mary Evans Picture Library. 11, 13, 26b, 29b, 30t, 31t — frank Spooner Pictures. 17m, 21, 27br — Eye Ubiquitous. 17b, 30tr, 30m — Royal College of Music. 23 — Lechner. 27t, 27ml — J Allan Cash Photo Library. 27mr, 31b — Topham Picture Source.